Women At The Well Cafe

Women At The Well Cafe

Sisters In Faith Speaking Their Truth: At A Spoken Word Table Talk

Marcia P. Samuels

JAYpublishingDen LLC

Published by JAYpublishingDen LLC
United States of America
Paperback ISBN: 978-0-9794526-4-2

DEDICATION

To all my sisters in faith

A Note to the Reader

Within these pages, you will meet familiar biblical women speaking in a contemporary voice -- honest, raw, and unfiltered. Expect spoken word poetry that feels intimate and bold, blending scripture-inspired truth with present-day language and rhythm.

The endeavor is that you see reflection, make spiritual connection, and revive your fearless, faith-embodied self for such a time as this. Knowing that regardless of time or circumstance, you are always relevant... for such a time as this.

Sisters In Faith Speaking Their Truth At

A Spoken Word Table Talk

Miriam

Mary Magdalene

Ruth

Hannah

Esther

Woman At The Well

MIRIAM (MC)

Good evening, family, and friends. Welcome to *The Women at the Well Café.*

I'm Miriam. You might've heard about my brother, Moses. To me he was just my little brother, but wow! I had no idea what God had planned for him.

You may or may not know this, but when we finally made it across the Red Sea, I led a huge celebration. We danced all night long, praising our God.

On a more serious note, I have my flaws. I got into a bit of trouble with God, and He had to set me straight. But thank God for His forgiveness. He listened when others spoke up on my behalf.

Here at *The Women at the Well Café*, you'll find resources and support for your body and mind, but more importantly, for your soul.

Tonight, we're hosting a special gathering. Five women, five stories. All focused on one powerful God. These women have come from different generations and paths to share their experiences through spoken word poems.

First up is a woman who knows what it's like to move from shame to purpose. Welcome, Mary Magdalene. **Reading:** *He Called Me by My Name*

Mary Magdalene goes to the microphone.

MARY MAGDALENE

He called me by my name.

Seven deep scars.

Let's just call them what they were:

Seven demons pressed into my chest.

Tearing my soul apart.

Keeping me in the dust of my birth.

Where I and other women,

Were just daughters of the dust.

Then He came,

He called me by my name.

Simple and clear, He said,

Mary -- just Mary,

And just like that,

The darkness folded, it squeezed.

It didn't want to leave, but it had no choice.

He who knew me best,

Call me by my name.

And the seven demons had to go.

Now free, saved, and with a purpose,

I followed Him because:

When someone looks past your flaws

And truly see you, you stay close.

You hold on to the love they offer.

You don't go back to the dust of degradation and loss.

I know you heard how I stood at the

Cross.

When others left, I stayed.

I didn't understand, yet I stayed.

And then,

Dawn hit the tomb like a mighty rushing wind.

The stone rolled!

The world rolled!

And when He said my name again,

O glory! Glory!

His resurrection was breaking all the rules!

Then He said to me, "Go tell them!"

"Go tell them" - - 'I am ascending!"

And so, I ran like truth had legs!

Spreading the word to everyone.

The world had to know.

He died and rose again.

I, Mary Magdalene, saw this for myself!

And so, I leave these words with you.

You are not what broke you.

You are not what left you.

You are the name called out of the grave.

When you hear His voice calling you by your name,

You'll know He is near.

Surrender!

He just called you by your name.

Rise up!

Rise up!

Rise up!

Jesus, called you by your name.

Mary Magdalene returns to her seat.

Miriam returns to the microphone.

MIRIAM

Shout out with me, "Jesus Called Me By My Name" Need I say more.

Our next sister knows about loyalty. Give it up for Sister Ruth, reading her story, STAYING WAS MY DESTINY

Ruth stands, and goes to the microphone, as Miriam, steps back.

RUTH

I STAYED

When true love came,

Though not of my people,

I answered love's call.

His love was enough. I felt safe.

Our future secure in each other's arms.

But then, the cruel blow of loss

Cut across our path.

When death without warning

Snatched my forever love out of my arms.

Loneliness wrapped itself around me,

Like a blanket, which could not keep me warm.

It would have been easy.

To go back home to family and friends.

Afterall, I was a young woman now on my own.

A childless widow

Where else did I belong,

But back in my mother's loving embrace.

Buth then something happened...

That changed everything.

This woman... A woman I barely knew.

Briefly joined not by blood,

But by the love I shared with her son.

She embraced me and wished me best.

Say it was time for her to return to her

homeland.

She thanked me for loving her son in such a

gentle way.

I tearfully said goodbye to her.

And then...I don't know why...

As she walked away, I heard myself saying,

Intreat me not to leave thee,

or to return from following after thee:

For whither thou goest, I will go;

And where thou lodgest, I will lodge:

Thy people shall be my people,

And thy God my God:

And so - - I travelled to a land I did not know.

Things were rough in this new land,

nonetheless, I stayed.

When tears flowed, I stayed.

Although I didn't understand all the reasons why.

My heart, my soul, compelled me to stay.

And so, I stayed.

I learned to pray to a God I now called

My God.

A God, who knew it was necessary.

For me to travel to this land.

And that it was imperative

For me to stay.

This God had already ordained.

That through my linage,

Kings would be born.

And the Savior of mankind

Would someday walk the earth.

MIRIAM

Thank you, Sister Ruth, for staying against all odds. From your spoken word, I'm reminded of Psalm 46, verse 10: *Be still, and know that I am God.* That's exactly what our sister Ruth did... she stayed.

And for those who may not know, Sister Ruth connects to Jesus through His genealogy. She was the great-grandmother of King David, from whose lineage Jesus descended, showing that God's plan of salvation was in motion from the foundation of the world.

Next up, please welcome to the stage a sister who truly knows the meaning of waiting. Please welcome our own Sister Mother... Hannah.

Hannah goes to the microphone.

HANNAH

Sometimes it's easier to say.

Wait on the Lord, than to actually wait.

Waiting takes faith, courage, and strength.

And yes, in your faithful waiting,

Doubt will creep in.

To wait means standing firm,

But also risking a fall.

I waited.

Watching the years pass by.

With each day...

Nature reminded me,

you're getting too old.

Still, I waited, and I prayed without ceasing.

I heard the whispers calling me barren.

But above the whispers

I knew God heard my prayers.

In my prayers, I heard a voice call me,

"Mother."

The voice was just a whisper,

but I heard it loud and clear,
"Mother."
And when God was ready,
I looked into my son's face
And whispered,
I am mother.

So, to every woman still waiting,
Your Samuel is on the way.
(Softly)
I am Hannah.
I was always meant to be a mother,
It just wasn't the right time for him to
arrive.

Miriam goes to the microphone.

MIRIAM

Thank you, Sister Hannah, for your resilience. You've shown us that the strength of prayer and faith, even when the answer takes time, is always worth the wait. God's timing is never too late.

Yes... it is so sweet to trust God. Just to take Him at His word. Amen.

Next, we welcome to the stage a brave woman. A fighter. A fearless warrior. She may tell you she is none of these things... but as you listen to her story, you'll agree.

This young woman's story, as it was then, is still true today. For such a time as this. Please welcome Sister Queen Esther.

Esther goes to the microphone

ESTHER

I was not born for the spotlight.

 I did not wear the finest silks.

I was a girl who played in the dust.

Tucked away between ordinary days and

the quiet fight for survival.

But destiny...

Destiny has a way of calling.

And when the moment came.

when darkened sky overshadowed my people.

When death walked with arrogant footsteps.

Destiny rose inside me!

Something fierce...

Something sacred.

I heard my uncle's words.

"Who knows if you were born for

such a time as this?"

It was then that I realized

Purpose is not polite!

Destiny does not speak softly!

Courage is an armor you put on,

while your knees are still shaking.

So, I demanded to see the king.

Not fearless, but faithful.

Willing to perish.

If that is my fate.

Destiny, spoke...Not me!

If I perish! I perish!

 But I must see the king.

And so:

I stood before the throne with

the quiver of a woman who has

everything to lose.

And a whole nation to protect.

And when the king extended his scepter,

I understood:

Sometimes power bows

When purpose stands tall.

My story is not ancient history.

It is a mirror of the past,

And A reality of today.

Today, I see women rising.

Embracing the joys and tears.

The failures, the victories of their destiny.

Women who fight battles unseen

Yet morning, by morning,

New mercies they see,

Knowing all they have needed,

God's hand has provided.

Thus, they greet the morning with unbroken spirits.

I see women...

I see you, with your fierce, spirit filled voice.

You, who rise even when the odds say stay down.

You, who know in your heart of heart,

that God has called your name with intention.

You were born,

For such a time as this.

You are here, at this moment, not by chance.

But by design. By destiny

For such a time as this.

You are stronger than you think.

Not untouched by fear,

but undefeated by it.

Walk in the wisdom of God
and the fire of prophets.
Go forward knowing that destiny bends!
by God's own hand.

I am Esther, yes!
You are my sister.
So, stand up my sister
Claim your victory.
For such a time as this,
Rise!
For such a time as this,
Speak!
For such a time as this,
Shine!
You have already won your
battle...Victory awaits!
For such a time as this.

Esther returns to her seat, as Miriam goes to the microphone.

MIRIAM

Ladies, we appreciate you for reminding us that faith knows no bounds. Thank you for spending this time with us. We hope you find something you can apply to your own life. Now, before we wrap things up, we have a little surprise for you. People often wonder why we named the café, "Women At The Well Café."

For those who might not know, the name comes from a well-known woman, recognized through time as the woman at the well. I know you might be curious about her name. Well, my answer is that her name is "Woman At The Well."

You see, in the Bible, even what seems like a mistake is not. Giving her a name would have meant identifying her, allowing people throughout history to connect her to someone.

It was important for her to keep the title, woman at the well, because in doing so, she embodies the very foundation of our "Women At The Well" concept, which is that all women, no matter their race or social status, are welcome. And tonight, I'm thrilled to welcome to the stage the one and only "Woman At the Well." Reading her spoken word: THAT DAY

A woman, about in her mid-thirties comes from stage back to the stage front, as Miriam, moves back.

The sisters at the table show a reaction of surprise, as they quickly stand and applaud.

The woman, smiles and give a slight nod at them. The women sit as the woman, faces the microphone.

WOMAN AT THE WELL

Sometimes God shows up

in the loneliness moments of your pain.

That day,

I wasn't at the well searching for miracles.

I just went for water...Just for water.

Like I had done countless times before.

But that day, He was there waiting for me.

It felt like He knew I'd show up.

He, who was a stranger, in that instant,

He saw right through me.

But He didn't flinch.

He didn't judge.

He didn't look away.

Instead, He said,

"Give Me a drink."

I should've said a firm no.

But His voice washed over all my excuses.

For the life I was living.

Yes, like cool water on scorching hot coals.

His voice, his smile flowed into my very soul.

He must have really known I'd be there...

Somehow, He knew I came for water at noon,

When others waited for the sun to set.

I went out in the blazing sun.

To escape the scorn and whisper.

I didn't expect anyone to speak to me,

They never did.

But on that day, that man...

Glory be to God!

That stranger was there for me.

I knew this because,

He revealed my secrets, my sins, my shame.

Not in a belittling way,

But as if to say, that's who you were.

But today, I'm offering you a different kind of water.

I pour it over you. I cleanse you. Please drink.

This fresh water I offer you.

It is the living water.

Then right there, just from his words,

I felt that living water poured over me.

It washed me. It purified me.

Right there at the well that day,

This stranger looked past all my flaws,

He saw me. as the woman I yearned to be.

So, I ran to a town that had only ever known me,

as the woman I used to be.

I shouted! I screamed!

"Come see a man.

Who told me everything I ever did,

and still, He called me worthy."

Yes, my sisters,

Today, you've come to the well,

that will never run dry.

And that man, that stranger

He's here just like He was that day.

Drink of the living water,

And you too will say,

that on that day,

When I went to the well.

I carried pain and shame.

But I left the well:

Found!

Forgiven!

Overflowing!

Here at the well, He doesn't just give us water.

He gives us dignity.

He gives us love.

He gives us forgiveness.

He gives us salvation.

And today, just as I did thousands of years ago,

Today, you'll leave this well with a purpose.

So, stand on your feet, raise your hands.

She looks over at the women sitting at the table.

WOMAN AT THE WELL

Come on sisters, please join.

The women, goes to the podium. And join hands. They then raise their hands together.

WOMAN AT THE WELL

Now, I'd like every woman

under the sound of my voice

to repeat after me.

We are women of faith.

(pause)

Strong in love!

(pause)

Rooted in grace.

(pause)

Unshaken in hope

(pause)

Speaking our

truths

(pause)

At the women at the Well Café!

(pause)

And beyond.

Music swells.

Lights down.

"Her Voice in Scripture"

Miriam

From **Exodus 15:20**

Then Miriam the prophetess... took a tambourine in her hand, and all the women went out after her with tambourines and dancing.

Ruth

From **Ruth 1:16**

Where you go, I will go, and where you stay I will stay. Your people will be my people and your God my God.

Hannah

From **1 Samuel 1:27**

For this child I prayed, and the Lord has granted me my petition which I asked of Him.

Esther

From **Esther 4:14**

And who knows whether you have come to the kingdom for such a time as this?

Mary Magdalene

From **John 20:16**

Jesus said to her, "Mary." She turned and said to Him, "Rabboni!"

The Woman at the Well

From **John 4:29**

Come, see a man who told me everything I ever did. Could this be the Messiah?

*She is clothed with strength and dignity;
she can laugh at the days to come.*

Proverbs 31:25

PLAY PRODUCTION

Run Time: 20-30 mins.

CAST: (6 Women):

Miriam (mc)

Mary Magdalene

Ruth

Esther

Hannah

Woman At The Well

CASTING NOTES:

Any age group, however, Ruth and Esther be younger than the other women, with Hannah being the oldest among them.

COSTUMES:

Biblical or a more contemporary take would also be fine.

DELIVERY OF DIALOGUE:

Rather than memorizing the entire poem, Actors can, if they so choose, read their lines aloud while performing. However, delivery needs to be convincing, emotional when necessary, and should create a sense of realism for the audience.

SETTINGS:

A cozy, modern café. Setting, decorated to your own specifications.

A small table with five chairs (for the women).

• A single microphone stands at the front (for the MC and speakers).

Mugs, glasses, and bottles of water/juice

Women At The Well Café
Sisters Of Faith Speaking Their Truth

PART 2

Release Date: April 16, 2026

Feature

Deborah

Mary, mother of Jesus

Sarah

Abigail

Jael

Elizabeth

Purblisher: JAYpublishingDen LLC

Website: jaypublishingdenllc.com